... loves to read God's Word

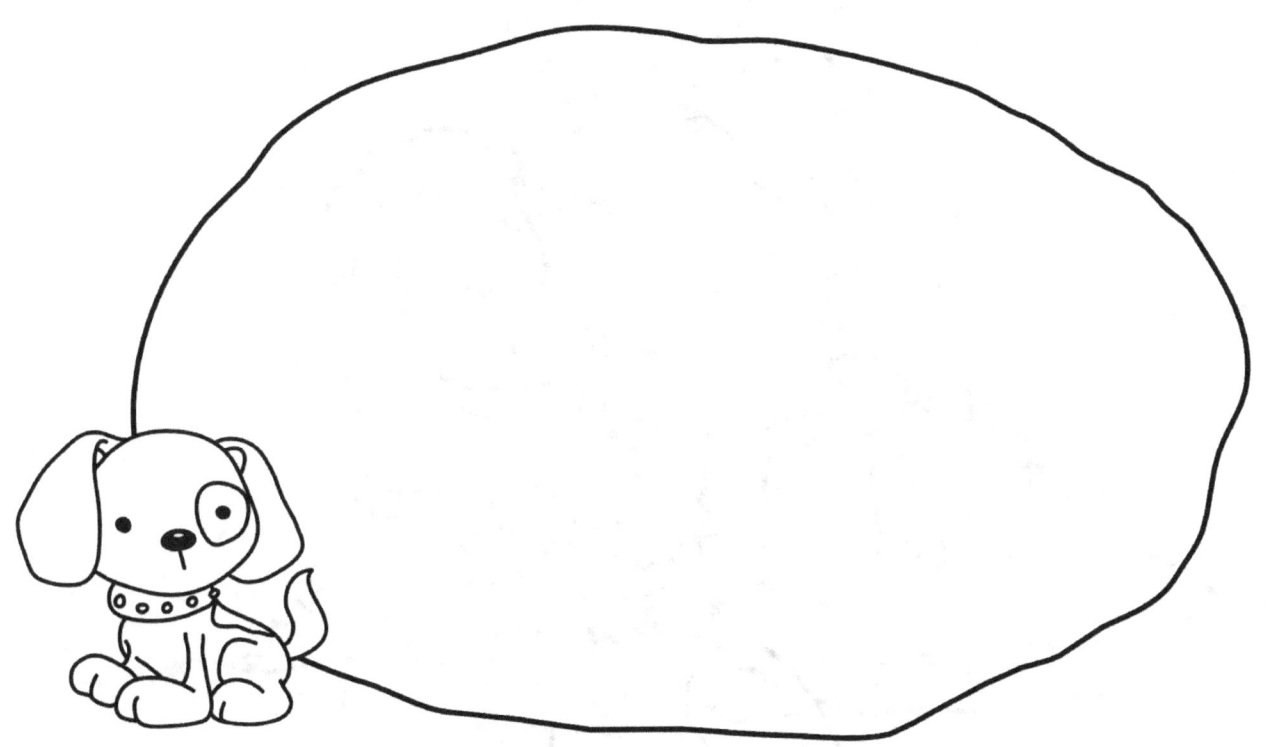

Draw a picture of yourself

Published by iCharacter Ltd.
www.icharacter.org
By Agnes and Salem de Bezenac
Illustrated by Agnes de Bezenac
Copyright. All rights reserved.
All Bible verses adapted from the KJV.

Copyright © 2015 by iCharacter Limited. All rights reserved. No part of this book may be reproduced in any form or by any electronic or mechanical means, including information storage and retrieval systems, without written permission from the publisher or author, except in the case of a reviewer, who may quote brief passages embodied in critical articles or in a review.

A King Is Born

Jesus was born in Bethlehem, in a simple place surrounded by animals. We can thank God for sending His Son into the world that special night.

(Read Luke 2:6)

Make the Same

Draw the missing parts for the baby Jesus pictures. See the first picture as an example.

Sweet baby Jesus lay on a soft bed of hay.

The Wise Men Visit

The wise men followed the star that led them to Bethlehem where Jesus was born. They knelt down to worship and adore Him. They brought Him special gifts to show their thanks.

(Read Matthew 2:1-12)

Find the Gifts

Help the wise men pick the right gift for Jesus.

Jesus at the Temple

Jesus amazed the priests at the temple when He spoke about the Scriptures. Jesus was a good student and the more He listened to God, the more He grew in understanding.

(Read Luke 2:41-52)

Match the Shadows

Which shadow matches the picture of Jesus on the opposite page?

John Tells of Jesus

John the Baptist baptized people with the power of God. He didn't care what others thought about him. He spoke boldly and without fear, preparing the way for Jesus.

(Read John 1:19-34)

Puzzle Pieces

There are 3 different puzzles on this page. Draw a line to join the pieces that go together.

Jesus Picks 12 Disciples

Jesus was very busy teaching and helping people with their problems. So He chose twelve men to be His special helpers. They traveled with Him and did everything they could to be of service.

(Read Mark 3:13-19)

What's in the Net?

How many times can you find the word "fish" in the net?
Color in each word with a different color.

Hanging out with Jesus

Jesus had a lot of love to go around. He was kind to everyone, from the youngest baby to the oldest granddad. He took time to make each one feel loved in a special way.

(Read Matthew 19:13-15)

What's Different?

Find and circle ten differences between these two pictures.

15

Water to Wine

One day at a wedding party, the people ran out of something to drink. "What are we going to do?" they wondered. Jesus wanted to help them. He did a miracle and turned water into wine.

(Read John 2:1-11)

Amazing Miracle

Go through the maze as Jesus turns the water into wine.

Jesus Calms the Storm

"Help! Save us!" called the disciples during a great big storm. Jesus got up and told the storm to be quiet. Then He said, "Peace, peace!" Amazingly, the storm ended and all was quiet again.

(Read Mark 4:35-41)

Put in Order

Draw a line from the numbers to the circles to put the story in order.

- Jesus took a nap.
- The storm stopped.
- The disciples were afraid.
- Jesus calmed the storm.
- The disciples woke up Jesus.
- The waves hit the boat.
- Jesus and His disciples got on a boat.
- The wind blew harder and harder.

1
2
3
4
5
6
7
8

Doctor Jesus

A sad father ran to Jesus, "Please heal my little girl. I know You can do all things!" he pleaded. Jesus went to his home and because of the father's great faith, the little girl was better again.

(Read Mark 5:21-24, 35-43)

Finish the Picture

Draw yourself when you've been sick. How did you feel?
Then draw whoever took care of you and comforted you through it.
Now, imagine Jesus visiting and coming to heal you. Wouldn't that be great?

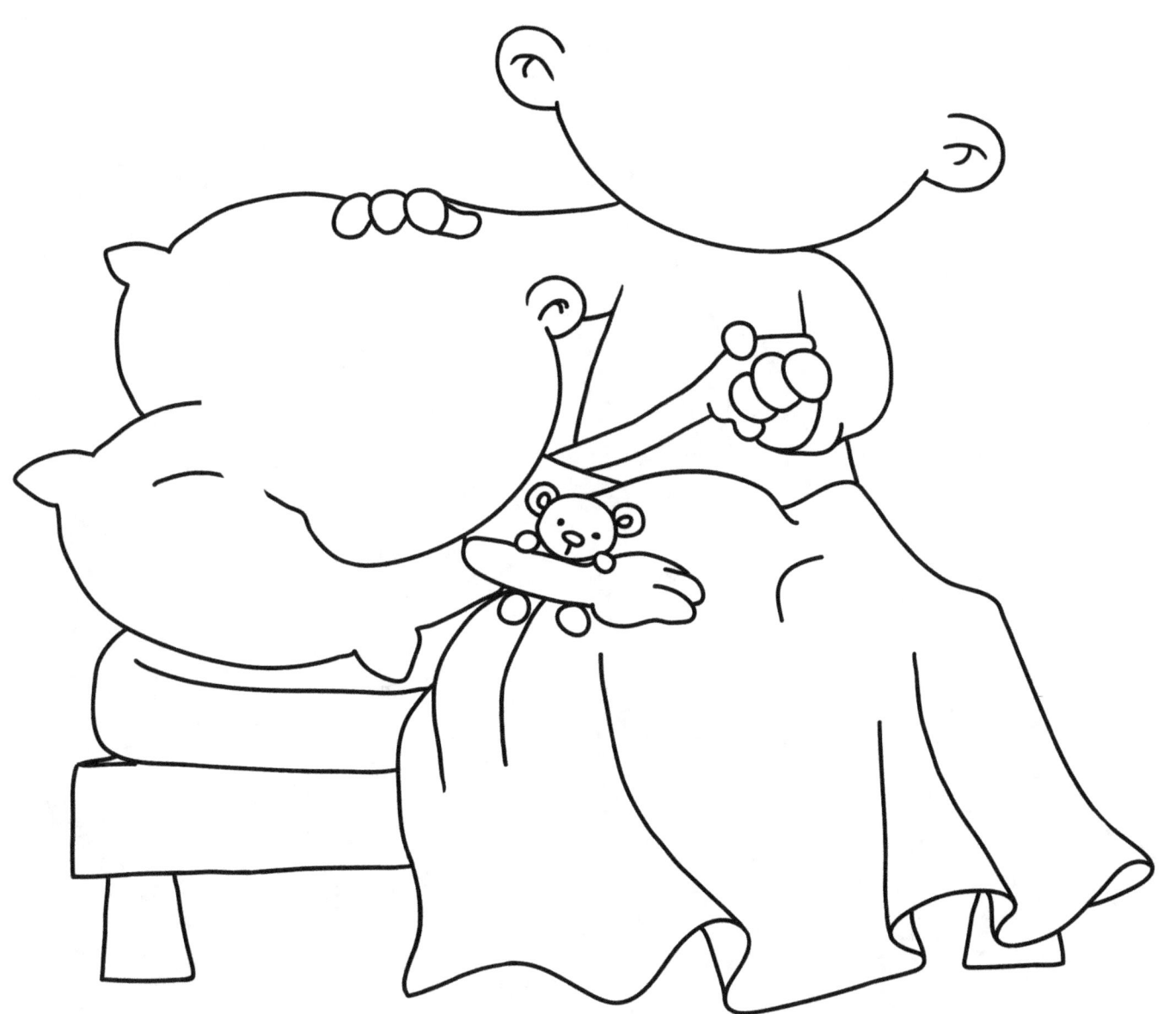

The Blind Can See

There was a man who couldn't see. "Help me please, Jesus. Help me!" he cried.
So Jesus healed him. The man saw the birds, the water and trees.

(Read Luke 18:35-43)

Make Them Glad

Color the faces. Then cut some "open eyes" and "happy smiles" from old magazines and glue them over the closed eyes and sad mouths.

A Lost Sheep Is Found

Jesus told a story of a shepherd who left his ninety-nine sheep to go and save just one that got lost. He found her stuck in thorns and he brought her home with love and care.

(Read Luke 15:1-7)

Hide-and-Seek

This lamb is playing hide-and-seek. Join the numbered dots to help find her.

25

The Lame Man

Some men carried their sick friend to Jesus. There was no place in the house and so they brought him down through the roof. Jesus healed the man and he could walk again.

(Read Mark 2:1-5)

Good Friends

Write the names of some of your friends in the boxes around the picture.
Then in the basket draw something that your friends did for you when you needed help.

A Boy Shares His Lunch

After listening to Jesus all day, the people got very hungry. One boy had a picnic meal with him and so he gave it to Jesus. Jesus blessed it and made it enough to feed thousands of people.

(Read John 6:1-14)

Moral of the Story

Find the matching fish and bread below and use the letters in each box to find the hidden message.

Stop to Listen

Mary stopped her work to listen to Jesus. But Martha got upset that Mary didn't help her with the cleaning and cooking. "Mary chose to put Me first," Jesus said. "That's the most important thing."

(Read Luke 10:38-42)

Guess Who?

Answer the questions by drawing a line to the correct pictures.

Who came for a visit?

Who is sitting still?

Who looks happy?

Who loves to spend time with us?

Who is working hard?

Who is preparing the meal?

Who looks upset?

Who should we put first?

Who took time to listen?

Jesus

Martha

Mary

A Samaritan

The traveler from Samaria stopped to help the wounded man who got robbed on the side of the road. He didn't just feel sorry for the man; he did his best to help him.

(Read Luke 10:30-37)

Follow the Path

Jesus told this story to teach us a lesson. Follow the path of letters to find out what it is.

33

The Party Boy

When a young man left home and wasted all his money he ended up with nothing.
When he returned home, his dad showed him love and forgiveness.

(Read Luke 15:11-24)

Put in Order

Put these pictures in the right order by writing in the numbers 1-4.
Then color the pictures and tell the story in your own words.

35

The Thankful Man

Jesus healed ten lepers who were sick, but only one of them returned to show his thanks. Do you remember to thank Jesus for what He does for you?

(Read Luke 17:11-19)

Hidden Message

Color all the letters in the same color that have the same style of writing.
Then find the hidden message and write it in the box using your own style of writing.

Zacchaeus Is Sorry

Zacchaeus was a greedy, selfish man until he met Jesus. He was sorry for the bad that he had done and his life changed. Now he found a better way to live by giving to others.

(Read Luke 19:1-10)

Word Search

Find these words from the story in the Word Search.

repent way sorry
Jesus money selfish
greedy visit give
better change happy

```
s a g r e e d y v a
t e w a y J h c i m
b r l l d e p h s o
g e h f r s e a i n
i p t a i u g n t e
v e u t p s w g u y
e n s m e p h e h r
t t s o r r y k z w
```

Into Jerusalem

As Jesus rode into Jerusalem, the people cheered and shouted for joy. They danced and sang and threw palm branches at His feet, as they did when greeting a king.

(Read Luke 19:28-40)

Clippety-Clop!

Sing "Hosanna!" as you follow the path to Jerusalem.

Not Just a Snack

Jesus and His helpers met for a special meal. He gave them each a piece of bread and a sip of wine. "When you eat and drink this, remember that I love you so much that I will give My life for you," Jesus said.

(Read 1 Corinthians 11:23-26; Matthew 26:26-30)

Find and Color

Find and color the pictures of the objects that Jesus asked us to remember Him by.

43

Jesus on the Cross

We have all made mistakes and done wrong, but Jesus had so much love that He died on the cross as a way to take our punishment for us. He made it possible for us to live with Him again in Heaven.

(Read Mark 15:1-39)

But Why?

Start the maze at the bottom with the question and find your way to the answer.

Jesus loves all His children. He died so that we could live with Him forever.

But why did Jesus have to die?

Write a little prayer here to thank Jesus for dying for you:

- - - - - - - - - -

- - - - - - - - - -

- - - - - - - - - -

- - - - - - - - - -

- - - - - - - - - -

- - - - - - - - - -

He Is Risen

Mary worried, "Oh no, where did they take my Jesus?" An angel said, "Don't worry. Jesus is alive again!" What wonderful news this was! She ran to share it with the others.

(Read John 20:1-18)

Wonderful News

Color and decorate this wonderful news.

HE IS RISEN FROM THE DEAD!

Jesus Goes to Heaven

It was sad to see Jesus leave, but ... "I'm going to prepare a home in Heaven for you," Jesus said. "And one day, I will come again to take all My children home to live with Me forever."

(Read Luke 24:50-53; John 14:1-3)

Odd One Out

Match each cloud with its pair. There is one that doesn't have a pair.
Which one is it? Draw a happy face on it.

Flames of Fire

The wind blew and a flame of fire that didn't burn landed on each one's head. "My heart is bubbling up with joy!" they said. This was God's Holy Spirit that Jesus had promised them.

(Read Acts 2:2-18)

Be the Artist

Draw a little flame of fire on each of the children's heads then finish drawing their bodies. Fill in the speech bubbles with how you think they might feel with God's Holy Spirit.

Good News to All

Jesus' helpers went everywhere telling others the good news of His love. From house to house, street to street and person to person; everyone needed to hear about Jesus.

(Read Matthew 28:18-20; Acts 2:43-47)

Many Ways

There are many different ways that you can be a witness to others.
Match the ideas and pictures.

I help pick up someone who got hurt.

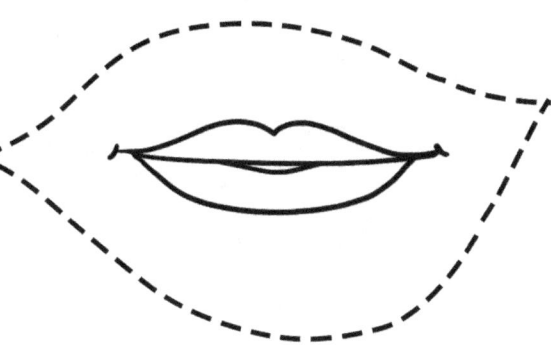

I look for the good.

I give a smile.

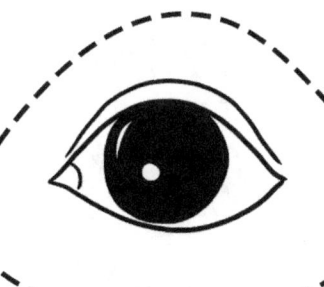

I answer when someone calls for help.

I go and find someone to cheer up.

Heaven to Come

John (one of Jesus' disciples) wrote about the amazing things that he saw in Heaven. Now we can look forward to that wonderful day when we'll live with Jesus forever.

(Read Revelation 21-22)

John's Visions

Illustrate some of the things that John saw in his visions of Heaven.

Answer Sheet

Page 7
1 = b; 2 = a; 3 = c

Page 9
Number 6 is Jesus' shadow.

Page 11

Page 13
The word "fish" appears 6 times.

Page 15

Page 17

Page 19

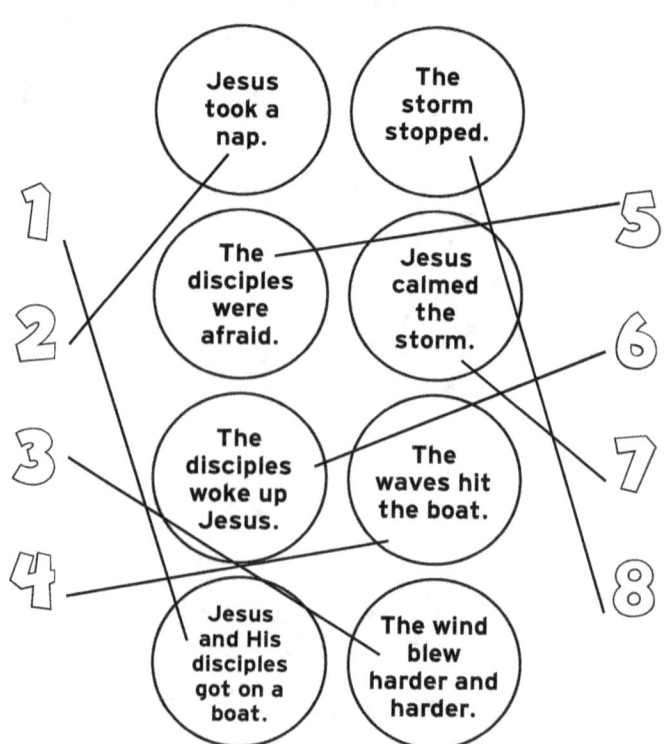

Page 29
The hidden message is "Give to others".

Page 31

- Who came for a visit? — Jesus
- Who is sitting still? — Mary
- Who looks happy? — Mary
- Who loves to spend time with us? — Jesus
- Who is working hard? — Martha
- Who is preparing the meal? — Martha
- Who looks upset? — Martha
- Who should we put first? — Jesus
- Who took time to listen? — Mary

Page 33
The lesson that Jesus teaches us is "be a good neighbor".

Page 35

Page 37
The hidden message is "Thank you".

Page 39

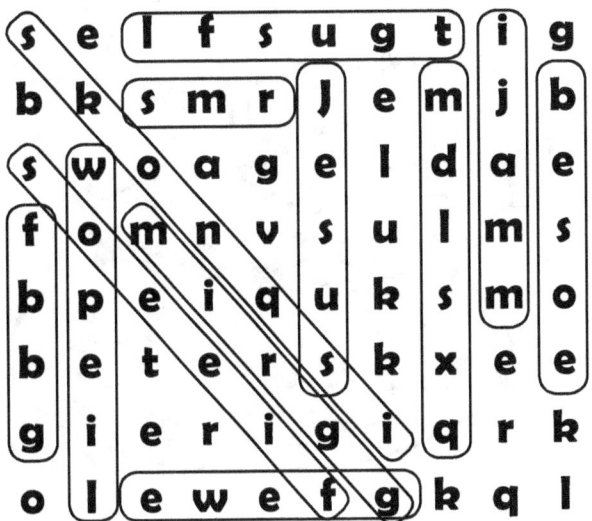

Page 41

57

Page 43

Page 49

Page 45

Page 53

iCHARACTER

Published by iCharacter Ltd.
www.icharacter.org
By Agnes and Salem de Bezenac
Illustrated by Agnes de Bezenac
Copyright. All rights reserved.
All Bible verses adapted from the KJV.

Copyright © 2015 by iChracter Ltd. All rights reserved. No part of this book may be reproduced in any form or by any electronic or mechanical means, including information storage and retrieval systems, without written permission from the publisher or author, except in the case of a reviewer, who may quote brief passages embodied in critical articles or in a review.